Flying on Her Own

Flying On Her Own

BY
Charlie Rhindress

FEATURING THE SONGS OF
Rita MacNeil

Playwrights Canada Press
Toronto • Canada

Flying On Her Own © Copyright 2004 Charlie Rhindress

PLAYWRIGHTS CANADA PRESS
The Canadian Drama Publisher
215 Spadina Ave., Suite 230, Toronto, Ontario, Canada, M5T 2C7
phone 416.703.0013   fax 416.408.3402
orders@playwrightscanada.com • www.playwrightscanada.com

For professional or amateur production rights, please contact
Playwrights Canada Press

The publisher acknowledges the support of the Canadian taxpayers through the Government of Canada Book Publishing Industry Development Program, the Canada Council for the Arts, the Ontario Arts Council, and the Ontario Media Development Corporation.

Canada

Front cover image: Alex Colville
Family and Rainstorm, 1955, Glazed tempera on board
Copyright A.C. Fine Art Inc., photo © National Gallery of Canada
National Gallery of Canada, Ottawa.
Cover designer: JLArt
Production editor: MZK

LIBRARY AND ARCHIVES CANADA CATALOGUING IN PUBLICATION

Rhindress, Charlie
Flying on her own / Charlie Rhindress.

Musical.
ISBN 978-0-88754-850-5

1. Musicals--Librettos. 2. MacNeil, Rita, 1944- --Drama.
3. Singers--Canada--Drama. I. Title.

ML50.R473F64 2008   782.14   C2008-903504-6

First edition: November 2008.
Printed and bound by Canadian Printco Ltd. at Scarborough, Canada.

"I worked through a lot of times with music, it took me through the good and the bad times. And to this day, it's certainly true."

—Rita MacNeil

Thank you to Rita
for living the life
making the music
and letting me tell the story

PLAYWRIGHT'S NOTES

In 1987 my girlfriend and I went to see Rita MacNeil in concert at the stadium in Amherst, Nova Scotia. We didn't know Rita's music, but we had free admission so figured we had nothing to lose. Sitting on metal chairs in a cavernous arena, we were transported. By the end of the evening that building was filled with a kind of love and pride in "one of our own" I had never before experienced.

As Rita sang a song entitled "Grandmother," my girlfriend and many others were in tears. Like so many of her songs it told a story and touched the heart. I began collecting her music. Every song a snapshot of a life; another scene in my head. I collected articles and interviews, while putting together the puzzle of this remarkable artist.

In 1993 I wrote and asked permission to write a play about Rita. Her management wrote back and said no. Taking Rita's advice that "we must never make a place where dreams will die" I kept collecting material and working on my play. In the fall of 1999 I thought it was time to try again. I contacted Rita's son, Wade Langham, who was by then her manager. They were interested. I sent a proposal. I met Wade in Toronto. I met Rita in Halifax. They gave me the go-ahead. And so began the journey (which entailed countless readings and workshops, seven drafts and three productions) that brought us to the script you hold in your hand.

So much of Rita's music is about sticking with your dreams and overcoming obstacles. Taking my cue from her, this play is an example of a dream coming true.

ACKNOWLEDGEMENTS

The idea that writing is a lonely business has not been my experience. Without the help and support of countless people this play would not exist.

I have so many people to thank. First of all Rita MacNeil. Her songs make my scenes live in ways that would not otherwise be possible. And that's not even mentioning her script suggestions and comments, which helped me get to the point of the story. She approached this project with an honesty that is rare and enviable.

Wade Langham for his willingness to consider my script proposal in the first place. Without him the play would still be twelve pages in a folder with a stack of news clippings.

Dave McClelland for once again reading my earliest draft and telling me I had something worth working on. Karen Valanne for reading every scene as soon as it was written, making suggestions and providing unending encouragement.

Brian Richmond for emailing, faxing and travelling from Toronto to make sure I told the story quickly and efficiently – in short, for keeping me and the script focused. Linda Moore, Jenny Munday, Ron Ulrich, Marcia Kash and Margaret Bard for providing dramaturgical advice as I struggled to bring the show to the stage a second and third time.

The Canada Council for the Arts, Playwrights Atlantic Resource Centre and Live Bait Theatre for providing funding support for script development.

And finally, all of the actors who gave suggestions, asked questions and breathed beautiful life into a bunch of words on a page.

The play is theirs as much as it is mine.

Flying On Her Own premiered at Live Bait Theatre in Sackville, New Brunswick, on July 20, 2000 with the following company:

RITA	Kiersten Tough
SINGER	Nancy Farnell Mooney
RENE	Gay Hauser
ROBERT (and as cast)	Nate Crawford
NEIL (and as cast)	Wally MacKinnon
BETTY/SARAH	Susan Leblanc-Crawford
TONY (and as cast)	Andrew Bigelow
CUSTOMER (and as cast)	Stephanie LeBlanc
Mrs. SMITH (and as cast)	Robin Lightfoot

Director	Charlie Rhindress
Musical director	Andrea LeBlanc
Stage manager	Krista Blackwood
Set and costume designer	Sheila Toye
Lighting designer	Paul Del Motte

A revised version of the play was produced by Neptune Theatre in 2002.

This version of the play opened at Live Bait Theatre in Sackville, New Brunswick on July 6, 2004 with the following company:

RITA	Krista Laveck
DAVID (and as cast)	Nate Crawford
SARAH (and as cast)	Meredith Zwicker
TONY (and as cast)	John Allen MacLean
SINGER	Nancy Farnell Mooney
BETTY (and as cast)	Jody Stevens
RENE	Gay Hauser
NEIL (and as cast)	Marshall Button
Director	Charlie Rhindress
Musical director	Jennie Wood
Stage manager	Barry Cook
Set, costume and project designer	Sheila Toye
Lighting designer	Paul Del Motte

ACT ONE

Two actors represent Rita MacNeil in the play, one is the person, the other her music. The person is referred to as RITA, while the other is called SINGER.

As the lights go down we hear an instrumental bit from "I'm Not What I Seem."

Lights up on RITA walking home from school alone. She is nine. FREDDIE, SARAH and JIMMY enter.

FREDDIE Hey, it's Rita MacNeil.

SARAH Hi, Rita.

JIMMY What happened to your face?

FREDDIE Yeah, looks like you're missing a couple of teeth.

SARAH Horse kick you in the face?

FREDDIE I think she's got a *hair-y lip*!

They laugh.

(chanting) Rita's got a hairy lip!

FREDDIE, SARAH & JIMMY
Rita's got a hairy lip! Rita's got a hairy lip.

They laugh. RITA suddenly charges at the boys. They get into a brawl.

SARAH *(stopping them)* Guys, Mrs. Farrow's coming.

They untangle themselves.

FREDDIE *(to RITA)* You're some lucky. *(rubbing his scratched face and running off)* She's strong for a girl.

They run off.

RITA picks up her books and wanders off towards the woods. She hums to herself as she walks among the trees. She starts singing.

RITA *(sings "Beautiful Dreamer")*

Beautiful dreamer, wake unto me
Starlight and dewdrops are waiting for thee
Sounds of the rude world heard in the day
Lull'd by the moonlight have all pass'd away
Beautiful dreamer, queen of my song—

> *She takes a Stephen Foster songbook from her pile of schoolbooks. She is looking for the rest of the words to the song. As she opens the book, lights up on the SINGER.*

SINGER   *(sings "I'm Not What I Seem" a capella)*

I'm not what I seem
I'm not what you're seeing
I'm a recreation of somebody's dream
Somebody's reflection
Somebody's pain
But it all depends on who's doing the looking

> *BETTY enters. Lights out on the SINGER.*

BETTY   There you are.

RITA   *(startled)* Betty! You scared me.

> *RITA quickly sits on the book to hide it.*

BETTY   Mom's been looking for you.

RITA   I didn't know.

BETTY   You're awful late gettin' home from school.

RITA   I was just here.

BETTY   Well come on. Father Murray wants to see you. He wants to bless your lip.

RITA   He always acts like he never noticed it before.

BETTY   He's just trying to be funny. Come on.

> *RITA tries to get up without exposing the book.*

What have you got there?

RITA   Nothin'.

BETTY   *(trying to get at it)* What is it?

RITA   Betty!

> They struggle and BETTY gets the book.

BETTY   My Stephen Foster songbook!

RITA   I didn't think you were using it.

BETTY   I've been looking for it all week.

RITA   I only took it yesterday.

BETTY   Every time I go to practise it's gone.

RITA   I'm sorry. I just love the pictures so much. Everybody looks so happy. I make up stories for them. Look. In this one, with the couple getting married, they've been sweethearts since they were fourteen. That's what I decided. Fourteen seems like a good age to have a boyfriend. And they're going to have six kids and live in a big castle in England. With a drawbridge and seventy-five cats and dogs. Happily ever after. Like in the fairy tales. And look at this one *(She turns a page and points between the book and her surroundings.)* Doesn't it look just like the brook? That's why I come here. I feel like I'm in that picture. I close my eyes and... *(She sings.)* "Beautiful Dreamer, wake unto me..."

BETTY   You've got quite the imagination.

RITA   Will you play the piano and sing this one for me?

BETTY   Maybe after supper.

RITA   I love it when you sing.

BETTY   Come on. Father Murray's waiting.

> Lights up on FATHER MURRAY and RENE, RITA's mother. RITA and BETTY enter.

Found her.

RENE   Where were you, Rita?

RITA   In the woods.

RENE   All this time?

RITA   I was singing.

RENE   Well, say hello.

RITA   *(very shy)* Hello, Father Murray.

FATHER   Hello, Rita. *(acting surprised)* What happened to your lip?

RITA   *(beat)* Joe Louis punched me.

> *They all laugh.*

FATHER   Well, considering you got punched by one of the best boxers in the world I'd say you're looking pretty good.

> *RITA says nothing.*

RENE   What's it matter what one little lip looks like when you've got a voice like hers coming from behind it? That's what I always tell her.

FATHER   We'll have to get you up singing in church some day soon.

> *RITA nods.*

Now, come here while I bless that lip.

RITA   I hope it works this time.

FATHER   Well we'll just keep doing it till it does.

> *As FATHER Murray blesses RITA's lip music comes in for "I'm Not What I Seem." Lights cross to the SINGER, who is still in the woods and will remain there for most of the play.*

SINGER   *(sings "I'm Not What I Seem")*

I've listened to people who've gone on before me
And I've tried to learn from the things that they've told me
But it all depends on who's doing the talking

I'm not what I seem
And I'm not what you're seein'
I'm a recreation of somebody's dream

Somebody's reflection, somebody's pain
But it all depends on who's doing the looking
Yes, it all depends on who's doing the looking

> *Lights up on RITA walking home from school.*

SARAH   *(entering)* Rita!

> *RITA keeps walking.*

Wait up.

RITA   No.

SARAH   I just wanted to say you're a good singer.

RITA   Oh.

SARAH   Sorry about the other day. Freddie and Jimmy are goofs and I kinda just went along with them. They pick on me sometimes too. 'Cause a my glasses.

> *RITA says nothing.*

I liked that song you sang at church today. I didn't know you could sing.

RITA   I do sometimes.

SARAH   I like to dance. I wanna be a ballerina when I grow up. What do you wanna be?

RITA   A singer.

SARAH   No wonder.

RITA   I was scared when Father Murray asked me though.

SARAH   But you were good.

RITA   My aunt Mary told me I had a million dollars in my mouth.

SARAH   Where?!

RITA   Mom said she meant I could make a million dollars with my voice.

SARAH   I wanna be rich when I grow up. And move to a big city.

RITA	You don't wanna live in Big Pond?
SARAH	No. New York I think. *(beat)* Do you wanna be friends?
RITA	When we grow up?
SARAH	No, now.
RITA	Okay. Do you wanna come over to my house?
SARAH	I'll hafta check with my mother first.
RITA	Okay, then come over. We live in the back of the new general store.
SARAH	I know. Your father helped build it, right?
RITA	Yeah, he's a carpenter.
SARAH	I'd love to live in a store. Do you get treats?
RITA	Sometimes.
SARAH	*(running off)* I'll be right there.
RITA	Okay.

> *Lights change as RITA enters her father's store. NEIL is there with ANGUS. When RITA sees ANGUS she turns and starts to leave*

NEIL	Hey, Rita, we were just talking about you. I was telling your uncle Angus what a good singer you're getting to be. Why don't you do one a them Stephen Foster songs for him?

> *RITA says nothing.*

	Oh, come on, Rita. You sing for your mother and me all the time.
RITA	But I…
ANGUS	It's all right, Neil. *(to RITA)* Maybe you can come by the house and sing one for me sometime.
NEIL	Ah, just give us a little.
ANGUS	Next time you run cigarettes up to me…

RITA   *(She looks uncomfortable.)* No. I'll do it.

> *She begins to sing "Hard Times Come Again No More"*
> *by Stephen Foster. Quietly at first but as she continues*
> *her confidence grows.*

Let us pause in life's pleasures and count its many tears
While we all sup sorrow with the poor
There's a song that will linger forever in our ears
Oh! Hard times come again no more

NEIL   That's my girl.

RITA   *(cont'd)*

'Tis the song, the sigh of the weary
Hard times, hard times come again no more
Many days you have lingered around my cabin door
Oh! Hard times come again no more

NEIL   Beautiful.

ANGUS   Surprised she can sing with that lip.

> *RITA looks at him and rushes from the store.*

NEIL   That's nice, Angus. Real nice.

> *Music in for "How Many Hearts." Lights up on the*
> *SINGER. RITA enters and walks through the woods.*

SINGER   *(sings "How Many Hearts")*

Some people hurt you for the rest of your life
And you never get over the pain they cause
It's just one of those days
You're up in the morning
And before you know it
A storm warning's come into your life
And it's not easy to ride
When your world's upside down
You can bend, you can break, you can fall

> *Lights up on RITA as she goes into the house. RENE is*
> *sitting in the rocking chair. RITA sits at her mother's*
> *feet and puts her head on her lap.*

And some people need you for the rest of your life
And they'll never forsake you and you don't know why
It's just one of those days
You're up in the morning
And before you know it
The sun is shining all over your world
And it all seems so clear
When there's love in your life
You can touch, you can feel, you can fly

> *Lights down on RITA and RENE.*

And how many hearts does it take till you find the right one
And how many clouds before the sun comes shining through
I've seen what good love can do
And I've seen the other side too
And all the reasons for calling love blind are oh so true

> *The lights cross to RENE and NEIL in the kitchen.*

RENE   I feel like I'm talking to myself most of the time.

NEIL   I don't know what you want from me.

> *RITA enters but they don't notice her. She is now seventeen.*

RENE   Someone to talk to. Someone who doesn't run away every time I mention something he doesn't want to talk about.

NEIL   Christ, woman.

> *NEIL exits. RENE sits at the table, then notices RITA.*

RENE   Oh, Rita. Would you sweep up for me? The boys ran through with their shoes on...

RITA   Sure.

> *They sweep and set the table in silence for a moment.*

RENE   While you're holding that broom why don't you sing?

RITA   I'm getting a little old for singing into a broom handle.

RENE	Seventeen and too grown up to humour your old mother.
RITA	*(bracing herself)* I want to move away.
RENE	What?
RITA	Sarah and I want to go to Toronto.
RENE	No!
RITA	I've more or less got my grade eleven and I'm not going to college. I can do the basics.
RENE	Your father and I never had the chance to finish but you kids... I mean with things the way they are nowadays you need a high school—
RITA	I thought you wanted me to be a singer.
RENE	I do. I just thought you'd finish school first.
RITA	If I go to Toronto there'll be a lot more opportunities. I can be a singer there, Mom. I just feel like I gotta get out. I don't wanna be stuck here...
RENE	*(beat)* Like me.
RITA	No, I just... I've been thinking about it for a long time.
RENE	Rita, the city's a hard place. You know what it's like. We were there for three years. That's why we came back. Toronto is just—
RITA	You loved it.
RENE	I loved working. But it wasn't good for the family.
RITA	Remember what it was like, working at Eaton's. Getting out of the house. Right in the middle of Yonge Street every day. I want to do that.
RENE	I understand, but it's so far.
RITA	I just want to try. If I don't like it I can come back. And I've got a place to stay. Sarah's sister, Joan, says we can live with her till we get settled.
RENE	You've already been in touch?

RITA   Sarah talked to her about it. Just in case we decided to go.

RENE   I don't know what your father'll think.

RITA   You could talk him into it.

RENE   Oh, Rita…

RITA   Please?

RENE   *(beat)* Let me think about it. Just finish the floor. I've got to get supper on the table.

> *RITA continues sweeping. RENE finishes getting supper ready. RITA starts singing Stephen Foster's "Oh! Susanna." She sings into the broom and changes the words to entertain RENE. RITA eventually grabs RENE and spins her around the floor.*

RITA   *(Sings "Oh! Susanna," adding some of her own lyrics.)*

I come from Cape Breton with my banjo on my knee
I'm goin' to Toronto, my true love for to see
It rained all night the day I left, the weather it was dry
The sun so hot I froze to death, oh, Mother, don't you cry

> *They laugh.*

RENE   Oh, Rita!

RITA   *(beat)* Are you happy, Mom?

RENE   Oh, for heaven's sake, Rita, sweep the floor. *(realizing she has never really asked herself this question before)* "Am I happy?" *(beat)* If you go to Toronto, promise me you'll work at your music. Don't waste your life.

RITA   I promise.

> *Lights cross to the SINGER.*

SINGER *(sings "Neon City")*

Standing on Bloor Street
Staring into the lights
Fresh off of the subway
Fresh into my life

*We see a projection of a city street. RITA enters in
silhouette and looks around, excited.*

*And if you could have told me then
What I could tell you now
We'd be the telling people
Behind the knowing crowds*

> *RITA exits.*

*I took a walk down St. Clair
My back against the night*

> *SARAH enters. She sees that RITA is not with her and
> goes back and pulls RITA in.*

*I met you on the corner
We danced away the night*

> *They are at a dance. "Neon City" arranged as a fifties
> number continues under.*

SARAH I'm so glad you came, Rita. We've been here six months
and you've been out, what, twice?

RITA Three times.

SARAH Three times.

RITA I'm just not comfortable...

SARAH We spend all week waiting on other people. The least
we can do is have a little fun on the weekends.

RITA I know. I want to, but...

SARAH I love the city. Frank's coming tonight.

RITA That guy from accounting?

SARAH Yeah. We've had about four dates.

RITA Really?

SARAH I didn't wanna say 'cause he was just breaking up with
Stephanie. But it's been a coupla weeks now. And we...
(makes eyes at RITA as if to say "you know")

RITA Already? Sarah!

SARAH   Come on, Rita, it's 1962. We're not living in the Dark Ages.

RITA   But… we're Catholic.

SARAH   I'll go to confession. *(spying FRANK and getting up to leave)* Oh, there he is. I'll go grab him and get some drinks. You want a beer?

RITA   Sure.

>   *RITA sits there looking around. TONY approaches RITA. She doesn't notice him.*

TONY   You want to dance?

RITA   *(looks behind her, then at him)* With you?

TONY   No, with my friend.

RITA   Where is he?

TONY   It's a joke.

RITA   Oh.

>   *He holds out his hand.*

TONY   Come on.

>   *She takes his hand. They dance. She is flying.*

SINGER   *(cont'd "Neon City")*

>   *And if you could hold me now*
>   *Like you held me then*
>   *We'd be two less lonely people*
>   *Trying to forget*

>   *As the song ends the lights change. RITA and TONY hold hands. He is walking her home.*

TONY   It's a beautiful night.

RITA   It is. *(beat)* I like your accent. Where are you from?

TONY   Sicilia.

RITA   Sicilia?

TONY	You call it Sicily. In Italy.
RITA	"Open Thy Lattice, Love."
TONY	What?
RITA	My sister used to have a Stephen Foster songbook with a picture of a man serenading a woman on a balcony. I always imagined it was Italy. The song was called "Open Thy Lattice, Love." Italians seem so romantic.
TONY	Some people don't think so good of us. You heard them at the dance. "Wop."
RITA	You have to block it out.
TONY	It's hard not to fit in.
RITA	Yeah. *(beat)* How long have you been in Canada?
TONY	Four years. Are you from Toronto?
RITA	No. We lived here for a few years when I was younger, but I'm from Nova Scotia. A little village called Big Pond, on Cape Breton Island. That's where my family is.
TONY	A girl shouldn't be so far from her family.
RITA	I came to Toronto because I want to sing.
TONY	You are a singer?
RITA	I'm trying. I'm working at Eaton's right now, but one of the guys there is in this group and he introduced me to his singing teacher. I've been taking lessons twice a week. And I'm gonna sing at a wedding next month. *(beat)* You're easy to talk to.
TONY	You're easy to listen to.
RITA	Thanks.
TONY	Tell me more. I want to know all about you. Do you have lots of brothers and sisters?
RITA	Eight of us all together. Five girls and three boys. I'm number five.

TONY   I like big families. I have four brothers and two sisters. But I think there might be more still. My parents are very old-fashioned.

> *He moves in like he might kiss her. She looks down at her watch.*

RITA   It's getting late.

TONY   What is it you say: time flies...?

RITA   ...when you're having fun.

TONY   Yes. I'm having fun.

RITA   Me too. *(beat)* But I should probably get in.

TONY   Okay.

> *They walk in silence for a bit. He stops and takes her by the shoulders, looking at her face. She self-consciously puts her hand up to her mouth.*

Don't.

> *He moves her hand and runs his thumb over her lip.*

What happened?

> *There is an uncomfortable pause as they look at each other. She looks away.*

RITA   I should—

TONY   Okay.

RITA   I enjoyed tonight.

TONY   I can call you?

RITA   Please.

> *He kisses her. Lights up on SINGER.*

SINGER   *(sings "Bring It To Me")*

> *There couldn't be a greater night*
> *With love all around me*
> *Around me so tight*

As their kiss ends, TONY walks away. RITA stands there, thrilled. He turns and waves to her. She bounds off.

Won't you bring all your love
Won't you bring it, won't you bring it to me

There couldn't be a safer place
With hearts so on fire
Nowhere to escape
Won't you bring all your love
Won't you bring it, won't you bring it to me

Won't you bring all your love
Won't you bring it, won't you bring it to me

Won't you bring all your love
Oh bring it, oh bring it to me

> *Lights cross to RITA and TONY. They are kissing. RITA pulls back. TONY tries to kiss her again but she pushes him away.*

TONY What?

RITA Can't we just talk sometimes?

TONY That's all we ever do.

RITA Let's do something else then. Maybe we could go visit your family. I would love to meet them.

TONY No. I don't think so.

RITA You said if we gave it time.

TONY Yes, that's what I said. Not yet though.

RITA When?

TONY Someday. For now, it is just us. I like it better like that.

> *He moves in to kiss her. He runs his hand up her leg. She stops him.*

RITA Don't.

TONY Don't what?

RITA   You know.

TONY   Rita, I've been waiting forever.

RITA   I'm just not ready.

>   *Pause.*

TONY   Do you love me?

RITA   You don't have to ask that.

TONY   Yes, I do. Because if you really loved me...

RITA   Tony...

TONY   Maybe we should just break up.

RITA   No...

TONY   I mean, I love you, but if you don't...

RITA   You never said that before.

TONY   I do not say it to just anyone...

>   *She leans in to kiss him. Lights cross to the SINGER.*

SINGER   (*sings "View From The Heart"*)

> *When I was a young child and rather early*
> *I had a feeling of being weary*
> *I was wise for my years, I was lonesome for my age*
> *I had a burning desire to be loved someday*
> *So with mixed emotions and a few kind words*
> *Some stolen moments in a brand new world*
> *I followed my heart around every corner*
> *Believing in love like there was no tomorrow*

>   *Lights up on RITA and SARAH at a bar. The band*
>   *continues playing "View From The Heart" under the*
>   *scene.*

SARAH   So what's the big surprise?

RITA   You'll see.

SARAH   You're not breaking up with Tony are you?

RITA   No. He's just at the bar.

SARAH   Shoot, you had me all excited.

RITA   Sarah.

SARAH   Has he taken you home to meet the family yet?

RITA   No.

SARAH   See, that's a bad sign.

RITA   His parents are Italian. They... you just don't understand.

SARAH   No, I don't.

RITA   Can we change the subject?

SARAH   Looks like we have to.

TONY comes to the table with drinks.

TONY   They're so slow I could have walked to the liquor store and back.

RITA   We've got all night.

TONY   Not to stand at the bar.

The band finishes playing the song.

MC   Hey, everyone having a good time?

We hear cheers. SARAH and RITA yell "Yeah."

Well, we've got a special treat for you tonight. The Maritime Club is proud to present a real Maritime girl. Where's Rita MacNeil?

RITA stands. There is some cheering.

SARAH   All right, Rita!

TONY   What are you doing?

MC   Rita, come on up here.

RITA   I told you I had a surprise for you.

SARAH   Good for you.

MC	Get up here, Rita.
RITA	Do you know "Hard Times Come Again No More"?
MC	If not, they can fake it. Come on boys, "Hard Times Come Again No More."

She sings a bluesy/spiritual version of Stephen Foster's "Hard Times Come Again No More." She ends up belting the number.

RITA *(sings)*

There's a pale drooping maiden who toils her life away
With a worn heart whose better days are o'er
Though her voice would be merry, 'tis sighing all the day
Oh! Hard times come again no more
'tis the song, the sigh of the weary
Hard times, hard times come again no more
Many days you have lingered around my cabin door
Oh! Hard times come again no more

The crowd cheers.

(to the crowd as she goes back to the table) Thanks. Thank you.

MC	*(taking the mic)* Rita MacNeil!

More applause.

SARAH	That was great, Rita.
TONY	She likes to show off for people.
RITA	What?
TONY	You like to be the centre of attention.
SARAH	She was just singing.
TONY	Yeah, I heard. I was brought up to think that women should not be drunk, singing in bars. But this is what Rita wants to do with her life.
RITA	Tony, that's not fair.
TONY	*(getting up from the table)* I need another beer.

He exits. Lights cross to SINGER.

SINGER (cont'd "View From The Heart")

> *My hands in my pocket and my heart on my sleeve*
> *I had a feeling that was way down deep*
> *I was eager for learning, I was learning to please*
> *I had a burning desire to find my dream*

> *So with sweet devotion and a candle burning*
> *I made my way while the world was turning*
> *And I followed my heart around every corner*
> *Believing in love like there was no tomorrow*

Lights up on RITA and TONY.

TONY How can you do this to me?

RITA It's okay, Tony. We can get married…

TONY I can't marry you.

RITA Why?

TONY I told you. My parents want me to marry an Italian girl.

RITA But once they meet me. Once they know about the baby…

TONY They've already picked someone out, Rita. It's all arranged.

RITA What?

TONY My family and her family… it's too late.

RITA You're marrying someone else?!

TONY I have to—

RITA But you said… you told me…

TONY We can do something. There are ways. Marcello, his girlfriend got pregnant and they—

RITA No.

TONY *(getting angry)* Rita, you are not having this baby.

> *Lights change. SARAH is with RITA. TONY is gone.*

SARAH   I told you he was a bastard.

RITA   He's just scared. He doesn't know what to do. His family won't let him…

SARAH   Rita, he offered to kick you in the stomach—

RITA   He didn't know…

SARAH   You're not thinking straight. What you and Tony are planning is murder.

RITA   We're not planning anything.

SARAH   I saw the mustard in by the tub.

RITA   I wasn't… Tony bought it. He wanted me to, but I told him this baby was coming whether he wanted it or not.

> *There is a knock at the door.*

That's probably him. Please don't start anything, Sarah.

> *RITA opens the door. A friendly looking police officer is standing there.*

POLICE   Rita MacNeil?

RITA   Yes.

POLICE   Constable Bigelow. Can I come in?

RITA   *(opening the door so he can come in)* What's wrong?

POLICE   Just something I'd like to talk to you about.

RITA   Is somebody hurt?

POLICE   Oh, no, nothing like that. I just dropped by to let you know that we received a call from someone who is very concerned about you. They informed us that you're expecting.

RITA   That's not against the law is it?

POLICE *(chuckling)* No, of course not. But this person also mentioned that you're... uh, considering aborting the child.

RITA Oh, no, I... I didn't...

POLICE Don't worry, Miss MacNeil. I'm sure it's all a misunderstanding. I'm just here to let you know that we're aware of the situation and to offer any assistance we can. *(handing her a card)* Here's a number you can call.

RITA But I...

POLICE I just wanted to make sure that you understand abortion is illegal. You do know that, don't you, Miss MacNeil?

RITA Yes, but, uh...

POLICE Good. That's all I wanted to say. Now, you take care of yourself. And that baby. Have a nice day.

> *The POLICE officer exits.*

RITA Sarah, did you...?

SARAH No.

RITA You and Tony are the only ones who know.

SARAH Rita, I swear...

RITA Then how would they...? *(She starts to cry.)* What am I going to do?

> *Pause.*

SARAH I called your mom. She's coming to get you. She'll take you home. Look after you.

RITA I told you not to tell anyone.

SARAH Somebody has to look out for you, Rita.

> *Lights cross to SINGER.*

SINGER *(reprise "How Many Hearts")*

And how many hearts does it take till you find the right one
And how many clouds before the sun comes shining through
I've seen what good love can do
And I've seen the other side too
And all the reasons for calling love blind are oh so true

> *Lights cross to RITA at the door hugging RENE. BETTY is with her.*

RENE   Oh, Rita, I've been so worried about you.

RITA   I'm all right.

BETTY   *(hugging her)* Hey, Rita.

RITA   Betty.

RENE   Nice place.

RITA   Thanks. Not real big but it's fine. How was the flight?

RENE   Good. A bit bumpy.

BETTY   Kept shaking and bouncing all over the place.

RENE   It was just a bit of turbulence. I love flying. It's always sunny once you get above the clouds. It was raining when we left but we got through the clouds and there was the sun. Just waiting for us. It's nice to know it's always there.

BETTY   I've never been so happy to feel the ground beneath my feet.

RITA   *(bursting into tears)* I'm so sorry, Mom.

RENE   Shh, dear. It's all right. We're going to take you home.

> *RENE holds RITA.*

RITA   I didn't mean to…

RENE   I know. I know.

RITA   I'm so sorry.

RENE   Don't be sorry. We've got everything all worked out. We've even arranged it so you've got your own room.

RITA   I coulda stayed here. There was a family…

RENE   You need to be around your own family right now, Rita.

RITA   I feel so stupid. I wish Tony…

RENE   You're not the first girl to find herself in this situation. Believe me, I know what you're going through. The last thing I would want is for you to rush into a marriage just because you—

BETTY   Yeah, marrying's about the worst thing a person can do, isn't it, Mom?

RENE   Maybe I'm different but I don't look forward to the day my daughters walk down the aisle.

BETTY   It's supposed to be the happiest day of your life.

RENE   Exactly. 'Cause once you're married it's all downhill from there.

          BETTY sighs in exasperation.

RITA   *(beat)* It's so nice to be around family again.

          They look at each other and laugh.

RENE   I'm sorry, Rita. It's your sister. She does this to me.

          The phone rings. RITA answers it.

RITA   Hello. *(beat)* Oh, hi. *(pause)* Yeah, they just got here. *(pause)* In the morning. Mom, what time do we leave?

RENE   Flight's at nine forty-five.

RITA   Nine forty-five.

BETTY   Is that him?

RITA   *(nodding to BETTY, then into the phone)* I know.

          BETTY takes the phone out of her hand.

BETTY   Hi, Tony? This is Betty, Rita's sister. How would you like it if somebody did to your sister what you did to mine?

RITA   *(reaching for the phone)* Betty.

BETTY   You bastard!

> *BETTY tosses the phone to RITA.*

RENE   Betty!

RITA   I'm sorry, Tony. She's just upset. *(pause)* I know. It's all right. *(pause)* Why don't I call you back? *(beat)* Okay, bye. *(She hangs up.)* Thanks. He was crying.

BETTY   Good. *(beat)* What kind of man gets a girl pregnant and then—

RITA   Betty, please. It's hard enough. I feel like… I've got this big empty hole in my heart.

RENE   It's not the end of the world, Rita.

RITA   It sure feels like it.

> *Lights cross to SINGER.*

SINGER   *(sings "Two Steps From Broken")*

> *Why does it hurt so bad*
> *To say goodbye to love*
> *And why does it take so long*
> *To finally see the light*
> *And why does the heart feel exposed*
> *Like a story the whole world knows*
>
> *And when love passes over*
> *And leaves you behind*
> *To deal with the hurting*
> *That fills up your life*
> *You're two steps from broken*
> *And you're one step from losing your mind*

> > *Lights cross to RITA. She is at her parents' home and quite pregnant by now. BETTY enters.*

BETTY   Hi, Rita.

RITA   Betty, what are you doing here on a Friday night?

BETTY   Just thought I'd drop by and see how you're doing.

RITA	Good. Mom and Dad are bowling. I was just gonna make a lemon pie.
BETTY	*(referring to RITA's belly)* You've popped out.
RITA	All over, it feels like.
BETTY	You look good. I can't believe it. My little sister's having a baby.
RITA	I'm twenty-two.
BETTY	Yeah, time flies.
RITA	Whether you're having fun or not.
BETTY	Ain't it the truth?
RITA	Speaking of fun, did you hear what Dad wants me to do?
BETTY	What?
RITA	Sing at a priests' luncheon next week. Look at me. Not married, six months pregnant and he wants me to get up and sing in front of a bunch of priests.
BETTY	He always liked your singing.
RITA	I think I'm gonna do it too. I figure what the heck?

> Pause.

BETTY	Have you talked to Sarah yet?
RITA	No, she called but I didn't call her back. I'm still mad at her. I can't believe she betrayed me like that. I asked her to keep a secret, then she calls you guys and the police.
BETTY	*(beat)* She didn't call the police.
RITA	What?
BETTY	I did.
RITA	You?
BETTY	Sarah called and said she was worried about you.
RITA	So you called the police?

BETTY	She thought Tony might talk you into hurting the baby and I didn't know what else to do.
RITA	Do you have any idea how scared I was, Betty?
BETTY	I know.
RITA	No, you don't. I was up there all alone and the police were threatening to throw me in jail. I wasn't going to…
BETTY	I didn't want to take that chance.
RITA	I can't believe…
BETTY	I was concerned.
RITA	It was bad enough when I thought it was Sarah, but it was you? And you let me stay mad at her all this time.
BETTY	I'm sorry, Rita.
RITA	Yeah, well you should be. *(beat)* Look, why don't you just go?
BETTY	Not like this.
RITA	Just get out!
BETTY	Rita, please. Listen to me. I couldn't let him…. The day you were born, the midwife took you, wrapped you in a blanket and handed you to me. None a them had ever seen a cleft lip and they were scared. They thought… but I took you upstairs and I laid you on my bed and I prayed, "Dear God, please let my baby sister live. Please God. I'll be good for the rest of my life if you just let her live. Please." And you let out this big cry and I knew you were gonna be okay. And ever since that day, my faith has never wavered, Rita. I know there's a God. Because he answered my prayer. He let that little baby, you, he let you live. So when Sarah called and said… I couldn't take the chance, I couldn't risk it. I couldn't risk that your baby might not get the chance.

Silence.

You don't have to forgive me, but please try to understand.

BETTY leaves. Lights cross to SINGER.

SINGER   *(cont'd "Two Steps from Broken")*

And when love passes over
And leaves you behind
To deal with the hurting
That fills up your life
You're two steps from broken
And you're one step from losing your mind
Now you're two steps from broken
And you're one step from losing your mind

> *Lights cross to RENE in the kitchen. RITA enters. She has not lost the weight from her pregnancy. She is dishevelled as though she just got out of bed.*

RITA   'Morning.

RENE   Afternoon. It's twelve thirty.

RITA   Really?

RENE   Yeah. Karen was up. I fed her and put her down for her nap.

RITA   You shoulda woke me. I didn't hear a thing.

RENE   Rita, you can't keep doing this.

RITA   I said you shoulda woke me. I woulda got up with her.

RENE   I mean you. *(pause)* Your father and I were talking about it last night and we're worried about you.

RITA   All I ever wanted was to sing and look at me. Five years after heading to the big city I'm right back where I started. With a baby. And no husband. And look at the size of me. Even my body's going crazy on me.

RENE   The weight'll come off.

RITA   I was a hundred and nineteen pounds when I got pregnant. You're not supposed to gain over sixty pounds. How can I ever be a singer now? I'm stuck here. I had a shot and I blew it.

RENE   It's not too late. If you want to go to Toronto and try again there's nothing stopping you.

RITA   How could I look after Karen by myself in the city?

NEIL enters.

NEIL   Lost another day. Thought we'd finish that roof but it just started pouring.

Silence.

Whose funeral did I interrupt?

RENE   We were just talking about Rita and her singing.

NEIL   Oh.

RENE   I was starting to tell her what you and me were talking about. That maybe she should go back to the city if that's where she wants to be.

RITA   But how could I?

RENE   We could take care of Karen.

RITA   You'd do that?

RENE   She's not a problem.

RITA   Just till I get on my feet. I mean, nobody could take better care of her than you.

NEIL   Look, you been moping around this house for four months. I'll go to Household Finance in the morning and get a loan to get you started.

RITA   You'd really do that?

RENE   As long as you're going back to sing.

RITA   I promise. I know I can do it.

RENE   You've got your dream, Rita. That's all you need.

NEIL   Well, the loan from Household Finance won't hurt.

Lights cross to the SINGER.

SINGER (sings "You Taught Me Well")

I remember September, the rain falling down
I thought the sun would never shine
I spent all my mornings, I heard all the stories
Of you and your days gone by
And while I was listening, my mind it was drifting
Dreaming of the rainbow's end

> *Projection of a city street again. RITA enters in*
> *silhouette. She looks lost and lonely.*

And in all my confusion somehow you got to me
And I'd have to say you taught me well

And how could I know the words that you said
Would come back again and again
I didn't realize when I was your child
Just how the story would end

> *RITA exits.*

And blessed are those you've loved and you've known
You may never see them again
But you know in your heart they all left their mark
And you only hope you do the same
But you know in your heart they all left their mark
And you only hope you do the same

> *Lights cross to RENE and NEIL. RENE is reading a*
> *letter to NEIL.*

RENE   "Thanks for the picture of Karen. She looks so big."

NEIL   She is growing.

RENE   "The music is going pretty good. I'm singing at the
Legion every weekend now."

NEIL   That's good.

RENE   It's what she was hoping for. "I started seeing a young
man from England named David Strickland."

NEIL   From England!

RENE   "He's a draftsman and he's very sweet. I think you'd
like him. Hope you are all doing well. Give Karen kisses

for me and tell her Mommy will be back to get her as soon as things are a little more settled here. Love, Rita."

RENE and NEIL share a look like they are dreading that day.

Lights cross to RITA and DAVID entering a restaurant. There is piano music in the background. A slow jazzy version of "This Thing Called Love."

RITA   Nice restaurant.

DAVID   Yes. *(handing her a rose)* Here's to four months.

RITA   Four months…. This music's very relaxing.

DAVID   I love jazz.

RITA   If we didn't have music no one would ever take the time to stop and listen to their heart.

DAVID   Who said that?

RITA   Me.

DAVID   I mean, who said it first?

RITA   I just made it up.

DAVID   You have a way with words.

RITA   Thank you.

DAVID   Do you ever write your own songs?

RITA   No.

DAVID   Why not?

RITA   I don't know.

DAVID   I bet you could.

RITA   I wouldn't know what to say. Or how to say it. And there are so many I love. Did I tell you I did "Wild Colonial Boy" and "Ramblin' Rose" at the pub Saturday night?

DAVID   No.

RITA   I was nervous, but the crowd really got into it.

DAVID   You shouldn't be nervous, you've got a great voice.

RITA   I wish I was doing more. I even lied to my mother about it. I wrote and told her I was singing at the Legion every weekend. She wants this for me so bad.

DAVID   Why aren't you singing somewhere every weekend? Isn't that what you're supposed to be doing here? You didn't move halfway across the country to work at Eaton's.

RITA   No, but... it's just so hard. I mean I want to be part of the music scene but I'm just... I don't know. I feel like I'm torn between two worlds. A big part of me is still in Cape Breton.

DAVID   You're here now, Rita.

RITA   Sort of. David, things aren't what they seem.

DAVID   What do you mean?

RITA   I mean with me, I... look, I'm sorry I didn't tell you this before... I've been thinking about it for a while now and there's something you should know...

DAVID   *(making a joke)* You're married?

RITA   Close. *(beat)* I have a daughter. Her name is Karen. She's only nine months old and she's with my parents in Cape Breton. I miss her so much. I think about her every day. I wanna go get her this summer. So if that's a problem I understand and we can call this off right now, but I had to tell you.

            Pause.

DAVID   Well, if we get married we've got a head start on a family.

RITA   You're not upset?

DAVID   I love you, Rita.

RITA   Do you have any idea what a wonderful man you are?

DAVID   I've got an inkling, but go on, tell me.

Lights cross to SINGER.

SINGER   *(sings "This Thing Called Love")*

When the night is calling
Calling out to me
I'm off to see my baby
Who's awfully good to me
Ain't no denying
This heart is buying
This thing called love

And when my day is ended
And evening comes around
I know just where I'm going
I know just where I'm bound
Ain't no denying
This heart is buying
This thing called love

Lights cross to RENE and NEIL.

NEIL   *(reading)* "Dear Mr. MacNeil, I am writing to ask for your daughter Rita's hand in marriage."

RENE   What?

NEIL   That's what it says. Look.

RENE   I believe you. I'm just shocked. It's awful quick.

NEIL   "We have been together for five months now and I grow more enchanted with her every day." Fancy way of talking.

RENE   He's from England.

NEIL   "I trust that Rita has told you that I am in a position to support her and Karen, who we plan to come and get as soon as possible after the wedding."

RENE   Is that it?

NEIL   No. "We will only get married with your blessing and hope that you will be as excited about our plans as we are. I look forward to your response. Sincerely, David Strickland." *(impressed)* Well.

RENE   Certainly sounds better than that last fella.

NEIL   Yeah, he took a helluva lot more than her hand and didn't even ask for it.

RENE   Neil!

NEIL   No, that's good. That's good for Rita.

RENE   Yeah.

NEIL   They'll be taking Karen.

RENE   Yeah.

NEIL   *(beat)* Gonna miss her.

RENE   Mmhm.

Lights up on SINGER.

SINGER   *(cont'd "This Thing Called Love")*

Now love is where you find it
Sometimes you find a lot
You wrap your heart around it
Don't ever let it stop
And if you don't abuse it
And if you treat it right
It'll be there in the morning
It'll be there in the night
So take it from me baby
Here's what I'm telling you
If you find someone to love you
Don't ever be untrue
Ain't no denying, this heart is buying
This thing called love
Ain't no denying, this heart is buying
This thing called love

    Lights cross to RENE and NEIL. She is making them tea.

RENE	Rita says Karen finally seems to be getting used to them. And she can say "Mama" and "Dada."
NEIL	She's talking.
RENE	They're moving. They bought a farm.
NEIL	Where?
RENE	A place called Dundalk. 'Bout eighty miles outside of the city.

RITA screams. Lights up on DAVID. RITA comes running in. Lights stay up on RENE and NEIL as well.

DAVID	What's wrong?
RITA	Go look in the porch. I opened the back door and it's covered in bats. How can I get to the outhouse?
DAVID	Use the front door.
RITA	I almost used the porch.

He exits.

RENE	It's a beautiful old farm house. Lots of land.
RITA	*(screams)* DAVID!
DAVID	*(entering)* What?
RITA	A mouse.
DAVID	Where?
RITA	It just went under the fridge.
DAVID	I don't see it.
RITA	There. Right there. They didn't tell us this house was already occupied.
DAVID	Guess we should have looked at it in the daylight.

Lights down on DAVID and RITA.

RENE	*(to NEIL)* There are lots of animals around.
NEIL	Sounds nice.

RENE   Getting back to nature, she says.

NEIL   I knew she wouldn't stay in the city forever.

> *Lights cross to RITA, exhausted. DAVID enters tired and sweaty. He goes over to RITA and puts his hands on her shoulders. She squirms so that he moves his hands. She is uncomfortable being touched.*

RITA   I'm tired.

DAVID   Me too.

> *Silence.*

I don't know how much longer I can keep this up.

RITA   You're not the one stuck here all alone every day.

DAVID   I'm just saying I'm tired.

RITA   At least you get to see people now and then.

DAVID   I'm not going into the city to have fun, Rita. I drive an hour and a half in, work eight hours, drive an hour and a half home, and then fix this place up until I drop into bed. Just so I can do it all over again the next day.

RITA   And what about me? What about my music? How am I supposed to have a career out here in the middle of nowhere. I'm back to singing to the trees.

DAVID   You wanted to move. Wanted to get to the country.

RITA   I know. But I'm a million miles from anywhere trying to clean a house that hasn't been cleaned in fifty years, taking care of Karen, pumping water... you have no idea what I put up with day in, day out. I walked out into the porch today and nearly had a heart attack 'cause there were two cows standing there. In our porch! We don't have any cows.

DAVID   Whose were they?

RITA   I don't know. They took off when I screamed.

> *They laugh.*

DAVID   We can't do this. It's only been six months and I'm almost dead already.

RITA   Now I know why when you die they say ya bought the farm. *(beat)* We're having a baby.

DAVID   What? Are you sure?

RITA   Yeah. I'm three weeks late and I've been sick all day, every day for a week. Almost threw up on those cows.

DAVID   *(hugging her)* Oh, Rita.

RITA   If I can ever stop vomiting I think I'm going to be very excited.

Lights cross to SINGER.

SINGER   *(sings "Southeast Wind")*

> *David and I collected old bottles*
> *Ladderback chairs and broken down rockers*
> *When we first came together we had such ideas*
> *Full of the future and full of good feelings*
>
> *David and I bought a farm in the country*
> *Tore down walls and planted tall trees*
> *Sat up in the comfort of working and sharing*
> *And planning a lifetime of living together*
>
> *Then a southeast wind came and blew up my mind*
> *Tore up the memories I'd long left behind*
> *Started me thinking and started me feeling*
> *But most of all it started me dreaming*

> *Lights up on DAVID doing some paperwork. RITA enters.*

RITA   Sorry it's so late. The meeting went longer than I thought.

DAVID   It's fine.

RITA   How were the kids?

DAVID   Good, but Kyle took forever to settle down so I've still got a coupla hours of work to do.

He gets back to his papers.

RITA   "And how was your night, Rita?" "Why, it was wonderful, David! Thanks for asking."

DAVID   How was it?

RITA   Amazing. I thought it would be five or six women sitting around talking about all the housework they had to do or something. You know, like a baby shower. But there were at least fifty. All these smart women, out there, doing stuff. Fighting for changes. It was just so, oh… I am so glad Sarah talked me into going.

DAVID   Well that's why we moved back to the city.

He goes back to work. RITA grabs a magazine and takes it to DAVID.

RITA   I mean, they pointed out so many things. Stuff I hadn't even noticed before. Like this. Look at this ad. Are they selling the car or the woman?

DAVID   I never really thought about it.

RITA   Exactly! Did you know that women make fifty percent less than men do? A lot of the time for doing the same job. This woman police officer from Sault Ste. Marie tried to fight it and the judge threw out the case saying that the difference in pay wasn't discrimination. He said the difference follows every rule of civilization and common sense. Can you imagine?

DAVID   I think I read that.

RITA   *(getting herself a beer)* They got me so fired up… I can't describe it. Want a beer?

DAVID   No thanks.

RITA   It's like these things have been there in the back of my mind my whole life and then these women said them. It's what I've been feeling and couldn't get out.

DAVID   I'm glad it was a good experience.

RITA   Good doesn't begin to describe it. I feel like my head's going to explode.

> *Lights up on the SINGER who sings a capella.*

SINGER   *(sings "Need For Restoration")*

> *Society made the rules and regulations*
> *Showing women how to sit, stand and walk*
> *How to wear their hair, catch them a good man*
> *And keep him ever by their side*

> *RITA takes a piece of paper and a pencil from DAVID.*

DAVID   What are you doing?

RITA   Writing a song, I think.

DAVID   *(surprised)* But you can't write music.

RITA   No, but I can hear it.

> *Lights cross to SINGER.*

SINGER   *(cont'd "Need For Restoration")*

> *So I found me a man in the good old tradition*
> *Being conditioned as I was*
> *But when it came down to making big decisions*
> *I found he overlooked my mind*
> *And there was unrest and a need for restoration*
> *To fill the needs in me*
> *To take command of my mind and my body*
> *And be the woman I could be*

> *Music continues under. Lights up on BETTY, SARAH and RITA.*

RITA   You've got to come with us, Betty.

BETTY   Oh, I don't know.

SARAH   You're in the big city now. Come see what's going on.

BETTY   I'm only here for a visit, Sarah.

RITA   Betty, it gets you thinking about so many things. Like, did you ever think about how when we were little the boys always got to eat first and we had the leftovers?

BETTY   Not really.

RITA   Women don't have to be put down to certain roles. We don't have to be trapped.

BETTY   It sounds interesting. But I don't even know what I'd wear.

SARAH   They don't care about your clothes.

RITA   Come with us. You don't have to say anything. Just listen. That's all I did for the first couple of meetings.

SARAH   You should have seen her last week though.

RITA   I wrote a song.

BETTY   What?

RITA   *(also surprised that she wrote it)* I know.

SARAH   She hadn't said a word all night, then Julia said, "That just about does it for this week. Anybody have anything they'd like to add?" And Rita stood up and said—

> *Lights change.*

RITA   I don't know if I can say it… but I was wondering if I might sing for you?

> *RITA is very tentative at first, but grows more confident throughout her performance. She rocks back and forth, keeping time by slapping her hip. She is passionate. This is music from the heart. She sings "Need For Restoration."*

Oh, when you hear them talk about the women's liberation
Be sure you understand…
That these are women, they're fighting for changes
To benefit you and me
And if you take the time, look all around you
Examine possibilities

Of how you could become more independent
And be the woman you could be

And we share unrest and a need for restoration
To set our talents free
To take command of our minds and our bodies
Fully sharing in society.

        The other women join in, clapping and singing.

And we share unrest and a need for restoration
To set our talents free
To take command of our minds and our bodies
Fully sharing in society.

        We hear the cheers and applause of the women.

        End of Act One

ACT TWO

*Projection of protesters at a Miss Toronto pageant.
RITA stands in front of it singing.*

RITA   (sings "Born A Woman")

*And the media, why they've done so fine
Exploited our bodies and they buried our minds
Follow their line and you're sure to be
Another brainwashed member in society
With a Wonderbra to improve your figures
And girdles designed to make you five pounds slimmer
Cover Girl to improve your complexions
Oh, don't offend the male population*

> *Lights up on RENE, NEIL and BETTY in the kitchen.
> RENE is sitting on a cot and looks frail. As RITA sings
> she walks into their scene and finishes the song to them.*

*And it was more than a feeling
More than in my mind
To be born a woman, you quickly learn
Your body will be their first concern*

RENE   That's something, Rita. It's great that you're writing songs now.

RITA   It's like I can't turn it off. I've been singing everywhere. Protests and rallies, a demonstration at City Hall—

NEIL   I saw them on the TV there, them women's lib ones, burning their bras. Is that the group you're into?

RITA   That's just what the media pays attention to. Betty knows. She went to a meeting when she was in Toronto.

BETTY   Yeah, not really my cup a tea though.

RENE   Your song, the tune was nice… maybe if you—

RITA   What?

RENE   Well, you know I love the western music…

RITA   Yeah, "Stand By Your Man."

RENE   I'm just saying…

RITA   I know it might seem hard to imagine, but these women… they talk about everything. Things you never even thought about before. Like being stuck in a situation where they're not happy. Feeling like they're not contributing in a meaningful way. And the movement is saying you don't have to stay in these situations. There are choices. You can take off. You can fly.

NEIL   Speaking of taking off, I'll leave you girls to it. I got some work to do around the yard.

            NEIL exits.

RENE   It does sound exciting, Rita.

RITA   Oh, if you could hear them. You would get so much out of it.

RENE   Maybe so, but as far as the music goes I think you oughta stick with country and western. You have such a gift and I really don't think you're gonna get anywhere with this women's lib stuff.

RITA   I'm not trying to…

RENE   I don't mean to put a damper on things but I've got to lie down for a bit.

RITA   Sure.

            BETTY helps RENE to lie down and get comfortable.

RENE   It's nice to have you home, Rita.

RITA   It's nice to be home, Mom.

            BETTY and RITA leave.

BETTY   Did you come home to help or what?

RITA   What do you mean?

BETTY   I thought you came home because Mom was sick and you wanted to help out.

RITA   I did.

BETTY   Then why are you going on and on about this women's lib stuff? You're getting them all worked up.

RITA   No I'm not.

BETTY   Did you see Dad's face when you sang that abortion song?

RITA   I was just telling them—

BETTY   I know what you were telling them. Give it a rest, okay?

RITA   I thought I might be able to share what I'm going through with my family.

BETTY   Mom has cancer, Rita. She can barely eat, it hurts her to talk. Maybe you could think about what she's going through. That's all I'm saying.

>   *Lights cross to SINGER.*

SINGER *(sings "Who Will I Go To See")*

>   *Who will I go to see after you've gone*
>   *I'm very fond of Betty and I'm very fond of Don*
>   *And I truly care for all the rest and I hope they do fine*
>   *Who will I go to see after you've gone?*

>   *Lights cross to RENE and NEIL. RENE is lying on a cot. Music continues under scene.*

RENE   *(waking up)* You been here all night?

NEIL   Yeah.

RENE   Must be tired.

NEIL   Not too bad.

RENE   You don't have to...

NEIL   Don't be crazy.

RENE   *(in pain)* Mmmm.

>   *He takes her hand.*

NEIL   It's okay. Just let go.

> *Her breathing seems laboured.*

RENE   Neil, I hear beautiful music.

> *She lets out one last breath. Lights up on SINGER.*

SINGER   *(sings)*

> It wasn't the place I know that kept me coming home
> Just to know that you were there was worth the miles I'd go

>> *Song continues as RITA enters. NEIL looks at her and
>> shakes his head. RITA moves in to hug him. As he hugs
>> her he breaks down crying. The lights fade.*

> Yet I truly care for all the rest, and I hope they do fine
> Who will I go to see after you've gone?

> This may be my last trip home, and the longest one I'll make
> And I'll watch the lines and the mileage signs
> I pray I'm not too late
> Yet I truly care for all the rest, and I hope they do fine
> Who will I go to see after you've gone?

>> *Lights up on RITA. DAVID enters and hugs her from
>> behind.*

DAVID   Kids asleep?

RITA   Yuh.

> *Lights up on ANGUS behind a scrim. We only see him
> in silhouette.*

DAVID   *(turning her around to kiss her)* So we're alone.

RITA   *(shaking him off)* I'm really tired.

DAVID   It's been weeks.

ANGUS   Rita, come see your uncle Angus.

RITA   I don't want to.

DAVID   Do you ever?

RITA   No, not really. I don't really like it.

DAVID   Well that makes me feel good.

RITA   Why is everything about you?

DAVID   I assume I'm the only person you're having sex with.

RITA   If it makes you feel any better I don't like it with the mailman either.

DAVID   Very funny.

ANGUS   Nine years old. You're getting to be a big girl, Rita. I think it's time somebody taught you what big girls do.

RITA   It's not you, David.

DAVID   Yeah.

RITA   It's not. It's me.

DAVID   Sure.

They say nothing.

ANGUS   The other little girls would be jealous if they knew what I'm gonna do for you, Rita. But you can't tell anyone. This's gonna be our secret. And when we're all done I'll give you a shiny penny to take home.

The SINGER sings a capella.

SINGER   *(sings "Born A Woman")*

Yes, something else had come my way
It blocked my mind and took away
The confidence to just be me
And see me through my day
And it was more than a feeling
More than in my mind
To be born a woman, you quickly learn
Your body will be their first concern

RITA   I think we should go to therapy.

DAVID   So I can tell a stranger what I'm feeling?

RITA   So we can save our marriage.

DAVID   Look, I understand a marriage is work. We're working. I'm not going for outside help.

RITA   I've got so much going on in my head and you say, "Yeah, that's good. Good for you, Rita," but you don't tell me what you're really thinking. You don't really respond.

> *DAVID turns away from her, tired of having this fight. Lights up on RENE and NEIL in another part of the stage.*

RITA & RENE
I feel like I'm talking to myself most of the time.

DAVID & NEIL
I don't know what you want from me.

> *DAVID walks off. RITA turns to watch her parents.*

RENE   Someone to talk to. Someone who doesn't run away every time I mention something he doesn't want to talk about.

NEIL   Christ, woman.

> *NEIL exits. RENE sits alone at the table looking defeated. RITA goes to the table. RENE does not hear her.*

RITA   Mom, I miss you so much. I spend half the time crying for you and the other half crying for myself. I pushed so much to the back of my head for so long, and now it's all out there, coming after me, pushing me right over the edge. I need to talk to you... tell you... needed to tell you. *(pause)* Uncle Angus... for years... in that big old dark house of his... those stained fingers, that dirty brown couch... and I wanted to tell you. But...

> *RITA looks at RENE who can't hear her. RENE gets up and leaves. Lights out on ANGUS. As the music for "Dream Forever" begins RITA sits daydreaming. The SINGER sings to her. RITA does not hear. The song starts simply and builds.*

SINGER   (sings "Dream Forever")

> Why is this world so torn
> Is there a better day, 'round the corner
> Take off and seize the day, some things we may not change
> We must never, make a place, where dreams will die
> Or lose our hope, oh, we must try to save the child within us

> RITA exits.

> There is a part of life
> We may not understand, we are shaken
> Cut as the heart can be, it only goes so deep
> We must never, make a place, where dreams will die
> Or lose our hope, oh, we must try to save the child within us

> I have a dream, I have a journey
> Whatever the cost, it won't be easy
> But if you and I start together
> I know that we can dream forever

> The lights cross to DAVID. RITA enters.

RITA   What are you working on?

DAVID   An old radio.

RITA   Be nice to see you upstairs sometimes.

DAVID   I was just...

RITA   Hiding in the basement. You should put a cot down here.

DAVID   What's the matter?

RITA   I want to talk.

DAVID   Okay... (go ahead)

RITA   I want to go home.

DAVID   What?

RITA   I want to move home. Ever since Mom, I... I just... I was talking to Betty today and I don't know. Life seems like it might be simpler there, David. And I could help keep an eye on Dad...

DAVID   What about your music?

RITA   It's not like I've got a busy career here.

DAVID   But Cape Breton? What would I do?

RITA   We don't have to go to Big Pond. We could live in Sydney. You could find something. I'd love to get the kids outta this city.

DAVID   Rita, I don't know.

RITA   Well I can't stay here. There are just too many distractions. Sometimes I feel like I'm two people. This singer, sharing her ideas with people. Someone who's got something to say. Things she needs to say. And then there's this woman who spends her days doing housework. I don't know who I am. I mean, I want to sing, but what does it mean for the rest of my life?

DAVID   You're just depressed.

RITA   I know I'm depressed. That's what I'm trying to tell you. I need a change. This house is starting to feel like a prison. This city… let's get away. I want this marriage to work, David. Maybe around family… when we were home for summer vacation… things just seemed like they might be easier there. Betty and Carol, they're not always searching. They seem happy.

Lights cross to SINGER.

SINGER   *(sings "Realized Your Dreams")*

So you never left the small town
With your friends when things got way down
You stood between the tall trees
Threw all caution to the cool breeze
And you stayed home on the island
And you watched the evening sunrise
And you never thought of leaving
Even when the winds blew cold

All you want or ever needed
You found here without leaving

It's the drifter and the dreamer
Who often fail to see
In the heart that never wanders
Lies a peace that comes with morning
It's knowing when the day is done
You've realized your dreams

> *Lights up on RITA drinking a beer and writing a song.*
> *SARAH enters.*

SARAH What are you doing?

RITA Writing a song.

SARAH I mean with the beer.

RITA Oh, you want one?

SARAH It's ten in the morning.

RITA You like wine better this time of day?

SARAH You're sitting alone, drinking at ten in the morning.

RITA I wouldn't be alone if you'd drink with me.

SARAH *(giving up)* Ahh. *(beat)* What's the song about?

RITA Cape Breton. I've been missing home. Writing about it makes me feel better. *(beat)* We're moving back.

SARAH What?

RITA David's going ahead to start looking for a job and a place to live.

SARAH How about recording an album first?

RITA Yeah, sure, you book the studio time.

SARAH I did.

RITA What?

SARAH That's why I'm here.

RITA What are you talking about?

SARAH   You're going to record an album. It's all arranged. Susan and Beth and I have been working on it and we've got everything taken care of. We priced the studio time, the pressing of the album. We even found a musical director. The money's all raised. You're going into the studio, Rita. So you better get picking some songs.

RITA   Are you serious?

SARAH   Introducing, Canada's newest recording artist, Rita MacNeil.

RITA   Oh my God. You're not just saying this to cheer me up?

SARAH   Yeah, it's a big joke, go back to your beer. *(beat)* No, it's for real, Rita.

RITA   I've dreamt about this my whole life. When I was little, if Dad was away on a job, I'd crawl in bed with Mom and we'd listen to these far away radio stations. And she'd say, "Someday you'll be on the radio, Rita. You're gonna be a singer." She always believed…

> *We hear a little bit of "Reason To Believe," which fades into the band warming up, tuning their instruments. Lights change. RITA is in a studio.*

PRODUCER
   I don't really know your music but I hear it's wonderful. Powerful stuff.

RITA   Thanks.

PRODUCER
   But none of it's written down, right?

RITA   It's in my head.

PRODUCER
   Do you just hear the part you're singing or have you got the instruments in there too?

RITA   Oh, I hear instruments.

PRODUCER

    A whole band in your head, this is gonna be fun. And for the ones where you don't hear music we'll go a capella. That means without instruments.

RITA   I know.

PRODUCER

    Well, no sense spending all day talking about it. Let's get to work. Why don't you just sing one a them and we'll start figuring things out.

    The producer exits.

RITA   *(into the mic)* This is a new one I've been working on.

PRODUCER

    (from the booth) Just go right ahead. Whenever you're ready.

RITA   Could you give me an A chord please? *(someone does)* Thank you.

    She sings "My Island Too."

The wind is blowing
Over your island
The season is changing
Your beauty to see
And although I'm not there
My heart is with you
...can this be my island too
...can this be my island too

    Guitar in.

I'd left you for profit
And high adventure
I came to a city
I never knew

    The lights change and full instruments come in as the SINGER takes over the song.

SINGER   *(cont'd with "My Island Too")*

> *The bright lights and the nightlife*
> *Have stolen me from you*
> *…can this be my island too*
> *…can this be my island too*

> *Lights cross to RITA sitting, looking at her first album, "Born A Woman." She is in Cape Breton. DAVID enters from work.*

DAVID   *(teasing her)* Just sitting around looking at your record album, Miss MacNeil?

RITA   *(laughing it off)* A friend of Betty's heard it on the radio and asked her if she could get an autographed copy.

DAVID   You're a star.

RITA   It's still weird. Seeing my name on a record.

DAVID   You deserve it.

RITA   *(beat)* I had a call today.

DAVID   From who?

RITA   A woman at the Mariposa Folk Festival. You know, that big one on Toronto Island?

DAVID   Yeah…

RITA   She heard "Born a Woman" on the radio. Said there's been a lot of talk about it. They're calling it Canada's first feminist album. *(beat)* She invited me to perform at Mariposa.

DAVID   Really?

RITA   Yeah.

DAVID   Well, if you want to go, go. I can take care of the kids. It's only a weekend.

RITA   She thinks this could be my break. I could probably start doing the whole folk festival circuit. *(beat)* If I was willing to give Toronto another try.

DAVID   You mean move back?

RITA Yeah.

DAVID But we just got here.

RITA I know.

DAVID Once we have our own place... we start work on the house in a month.

RITA That's why I was thinking maybe I should go alone.

DAVID Alone?

RITA Well, you've got your job. And the kids would probably be better off with you right now.

DAVID For how long?

RITA Just until I get the music going. Or I get myself a life.

DAVID You've got a life here.

RITA No, I've got your lives. You and the kids. And... I wish there was some way I could explain it. It's this emptiness. And I feel like I might be able to fill it. But not here. Not right now. There are just too many memories.

DAVID You're the one who wanted to come back.

RITA I know.

DAVID You can do your music here. You performed at the Big Pond Festival. There are bars in Sydney.

RITA It's not the same.

DAVID Rita, we've tried Toronto. You were there for almost fifteen years.

RITA But I've got the album now. It'll make all kinds of new opportunities. If I can't sing I'm never gonna be any good to you or the kids.

DAVID So you're leaving us?

> *Neither of them knows what to say. Lights cross to SINGER.*

SINGER   *(sings "Memphis")*

> *She was honest, it was over*
> *Love don't live here anymore*
> *No more searching for the answers*
> *When you already know*
> *She was willing, through the bad times*
> *She'd try harder than before*
> *For the light, she would hold on*
> *She's not reaching anymore*
>
> *And there is nothing sadder*
> *Than to know when love is gone*
> *No easy way of leaving*
> *And no words to make it right*

> *There is a knock. We see an AGENT in silhouette.*

AGENT   Come in!

RITA   There was nobody at the desk so I just…

AGENT   Yeah, how can I help you?

RITA   I saw your ad in the paper and I was just wondering if you're signing up any new singers.

AGENT   Got a band?

RITA   No, it's just me. But I'm gonna be singing at the Mariposa Folk Festival next month. And I have an album.

AGENT   We don't go much for solo singers. Looking more for bands right now. Why don't you try back in a couple months?

> *Lights up on AGENT TWO in silhouette.*

AGENT TWO
> Now see, if you played guitar we might have something. That whole Joni Mitchell, folksy, singer-songwriter thing is big now but not some chick slapping her hip singing a capella. Don't get me wrong. You're good. Just not for us.

> *Lights up on AGENT THREE in silhouette.*

AGENT THREE
> Well, you got a good voice. I'll give you that. But you gotta work on the look. Maybe lose thirty pounds, show a little cleavage. Tits work wonders.

> *Lights down on the AGENTS. Music for "Get Outt'a Here" under the scene. Party sounds. RITA and SARAH are drinking.*

SARAH Should you be drinking before you perform?

RITA I just need a little something to help get me up there. But I've only had two and I'm feeling light-headed already.

SARAH What have you eaten today?

RITA An apple for lunch.

SARAH That's it?

RITA I gotta lose some weight.

SARAH I can't believe you of all people are buying into that whole "a singer's gotta have a look" thing.

RITA Sarah, if I don't get an agent I'll be singing in university pubs like this till I'm seventy-five. And nobody's gonna sign me looking like this.

> *RITA gets a bottle of pills out of her purse and takes one.*

SARAH You're eating those pills like candy.

RITA The doctor told me to take one whenever I feel anxious or stressful. I'm feeling a lot of anxious and stressful these days.

SARAH Was he the one who recommended you wash it down with beer?

RITA Stop lecturing. I've got enough to feel guilty about.

SARAH Sorry.

RITA   David called last night. I talked to the kids. Kyle told me that Sue, that woman who looks after them, told him and Karen that their mommy left because she didn't love them.

SARAH   What a bitch.

RITA   I just… I want to go get them. I told David. I just don't know how I'd take care of them. I feel so guilty. I think I'm gonna get that put on a nameplate and hang it above the door. "Guilt." To hell with MacNeil. *(beat)* When I was little Dad used to go away on jobs to Newfoundland all the time. He'd leave Mom alone with eight kids for weeks. Nobody ever said a thing. But if a woman does the same thing…

SARAH   Yeah, but are you just looking for work, or are you leaving David?

RITA   I don't even know anymore. *(gets up to leave)* I need another beer.

> *Lights cross to SINGER.*

SINGER   *(sings "Get Outt'a Here")*

> *When I get to drinkin'*
> *Oh, I get to thinkin'*
> *On all the things I might have been*
> *But the could haves and the should haves*
> *Are all wrapped up in "I would have"*
> *If only for drinkin' this beer*
> *Get outt'a here*
> *Before you drown in that glass*
> *You'll sink to the bottom*
> *And you'll never come back*
> *You've been taking a snooze*
> *In a river of booze*
> *And the only way out*
> *Is to clear up your head*
> *And the only way out*
> *Is to clear up your head*

Lights up on DAVID and RITA entering. RITA is carrying a small travel case. They are uncomfortable with each other.

RITA   Wow. The house looks great.

DAVID   Thanks. Few little things left to do…

RITA   No, it's really nice. *(beat)* Thanks for picking me up.

DAVID   No problem. Kids should be home anytime.

RITA   I can't wait to see them.

BETTY walks into the room.

BETTY   Hi, Rita.

RITA   Betty, David didn't tell me you'd be here.

BETTY   I let myself in. *(beat)* I told David I'd come by and try to talk some sense into you.

DAVID   I told you—

BETTY   Why don't you stay?

RITA   I can't.

BETTY   You mean you don't want to.

DAVID   Betty…

BETTY   It's not just you you're hurting.

RITA   Do you think I don't know that?

BETTY   Why do you keep running?

RITA   I'm looking for—

BETTY   Someplace else to run to. Why can't you try it here? Or even Halifax if it's got to be a city.

RITA   I can't… it's too hard. David, I love you, but I just can't…

DAVID   I know.

BETTY   How are you even gonna take care of the kids?

DAVID   Betty, don't.

RITA   I'll find something. It might not be music, but—

BETTY   I can't stand by and let you throw your life away.

RITA   I just don't want to be married anymore.

> *DAVID exits.*

BETTY   He worked like crazy trying to finish this house for you. He's a good man, Rita.

RITA   And what does that have to do with me? Am I supposed to stay with him forever because he's a good man?

BETTY   Have you even thought about the kids?

RITA   Why do you think I'm here? It's almost harder taking them than it was leaving them. Because I know how much it'll hurt David. And I know how much they'll miss him. But I need them too. And I think they need me.

BETTY   Well I think you're throwing away a good marriage. It's time you got your life together, Rita. Quit running around. It's time to grow up.

> *Lights cross to SINGER.*

SINGER   *(sings "Southeast Wind")*

> *David and I gathered up our belongings*
> *Parting the ways when the dreams started falling*
> *We visit the children on separate occasions*
> *And justify loneliness whenever we're able*
>
> *David and I live in separate places*
> *And sometimes I run off to live in the spaces*
> *I sit in the rocker, set chairs 'round the table*
> *And bury my past with gentle persuasion*
>
> *Then a southeast wind came and blew up my mind*
> *Tore up the memories I'd long left behind*
> *Started me thinking and started me feeling*

But most of all it started me dreaming
Dreaming, dreaming, dreaming

> *Knocking at the door. We see a projection of a tiny apartment. Lights up on RITA in her bathrobe. She looks half asleep. RUBAN appears in silhouette only.*

RITA   Hello?

RUBAN   Hi, I'm Jeffrey Ruban from Social Services.

RITA   Oh, hi. How can I help you?

RUBAN   I'm here for a home visit.

RITA   I didn't know… no one told me…

RUBAN   This is an unscheduled visit. *(looking at his watch)* Did I get you out of bed?

RITA   No, I just… I was singing late last night so I got the kids off to school and then… the place is a bit of a mess. I wasn't expecting company.

RUBAN   Right. *(looking around some more)* These your shoes?

RITA   Yes.

RUBAN   Both pairs?

RITA   Yes.

RUBAN   So there are no other adults living here?

RITA   No. It's just me and the kids.

RUBAN   And you say they're at school?

RITA   Yes. They're nine and thirteen.

RUBAN   *(looking at his files)* I can see that here. And have you been looking for work?

RITA   Yeah. I'm a singer but I've been looking for anything.

RUBAN   We'll need a list of the places you've applied in the past two weeks.

RITA   I'll do that up and drop it off.

RUBAN   This afternoon would be great. Have you been to the university yet?

RITA   What for?

RUBAN   The career assessment.

RITA   Uh, no, I didn't know…

RUBAN   Someone should have told you.

RITA   Well they didn't.

RUBAN   You'll have to complete the Choices Program. It's a career assessment questionnaire. You fill it out, feed it into the computer and you receive a printout of appropriate career options.

RITA   Oh.

        The projection changes. It is a sparse white office. We see the CAREER ASSESSMENT OFFICER (CAO) in silhouette.

CAO   Okay, here are the results. It's an amazing program. *(looking over the computer printout)* You wrote that you like music.

RITA   Yes.

CAO   Do you play an instrument?

RITA   No.

CAO   Read music?

RITA   No.

CAO   What do you do?

RITA   I sing.

CAO   Oh.

RITA   And I write my own songs.

CAO   Well, according to this you have little or no aptitude for a musical career. That's too bad. But it does say you could probably succeed at nursing. Or maybe as a home-care worker.

Lights change. It is a doctor's office. We now see the THERAPIST in silhouette.

THERAPIST
So, how are things this week?

RITA   I've messed everything up so bad. Karen's really missing her school back home. She just gets settled and I make her move again... I can see it in her eyes. She looked at me the other day and I could swear I was looking into my mother's eyes. They showed these... these glimpses of pain. I did to her what my father did to my mother. And I'm just... I was swimming every day. I lost fifty pounds, I was down to one thirty-five, but then it started coming back on and, and... I know it doesn't really matter, but it's just another thing that I can't control and... I... I just can't stop crying. I... my whole life is out of control. Everything hurts so much.

Lights up on the SINGER who sings a capella. RITA picks up a bottle of pills and a glass of water and sits on the side of her bed. During the song she swallows a handful of pills, then curls up on the bed and the lights fade on her.

SINGER   *(sings "I Have A Son... I Have A Daughter")*

I have a son and I have a daughter
And I hope they come into something better
I've been around trying to find
What makes this world of ours survive
You would think with all you see
There'd be enough for you and for me
But the scales of justice are out of whack
They're using salt and rocky sand

We hear two children's voices.

KYLE   Mommy!

KAREN   Wake up!

KYLE   Mommy, what's wrong?

SINGER   *(cont'd "I Have A Son... I Have A Daughter")*

> *You give your trust to those in power*
> *In the hopes of something better*
> *Then like a child who's been betrayed*
> *You'll turn your backs on all they say*

>> *Lights up dimly on RITA on the bed with KAREN and KYLE. Music continues under.*

RITA   *(coming around)* Oh my God.

KYLE   Mommy's awake.

KAREN   You were sleeping so hard we couldn't wake you up.

RITA   How long was I asleep?

KAREN   Since yesterday.

RITA   What?

KAREN   It's Saturday.

RITA   Really?

KAREN   Yuh, cartoon day.

RITA   Oh no. Oh, I'm sorry. Come here. *(She hugs them.)* I'm so sorry.

KYLE   It's all right. We had pizza.

> *She holds them as the lights fade.*

SINGER   *(cont'd "I Have A Son... I Have A Daughter")*

> *I have a son and I have a daughter*
> *And I hope they come into something better*
> *I've been around trying to find*
> *What makes this world of ours survive*

>> *Lights up on RITA. She is sweeping. An instrumental bit from "Reason To Believe" begins. RENE appears.*

RENE   While you're holding that broom why don't you sing?

RITA turns to see her mother.

RITA Mom?

RENE What were you thinking, Rita?

RITA About everything. *(pause)* It just seemed easier than carrying on.

RENE What about those kids? How could you do that to them?

RITA I'm a single mother on welfare, cleaning strangers' houses for a few extra bucks. I've been waiting thirty-five years for life to start and I suddenly realized, maybe this is it. This is how it's gonna be. It hasn't just started, it's half over.

RENE What happened to the dream?

RITA I'm scared of it. Most of the time I can barely walk out on the stage I'm so scared. It's like somebody who's afraid of heights dreaming of being a skydiver.

RENE Do you still want it?

RITA I think so. But I don't know how to make it happen. And I'm so tired. Tired of always looking for something. A sense of peace. Home.

RENE Why don't you go home?

RITA I don't know that Cape Breton is... I've tried... there are just too many memories.

Pause.

RENE It's not your fault, Rita. You were a little girl.

RITA I keep going back looking for her. I want to find that little girl and take her in my arms and tell her it's going to be all right.

RENE It *is* going to be all right.

RITA I don't know anymore. I don't know what to do next. I don't know what the right thing is.

RENE   What about that woman who wanted you to sing at the Women's Day celebrations in Sydney? Why don't you do that?

RITA   I don't know.

RENE   Yes you do, Rita.

> *Lights cross to SINGER.*

SINGER   (*sings "Reason To Believe"*)

> *I've been going over my life*
> *And I feel you in the breeze*
> *You're a constant reminder*
> *Of what used to be*
> *And I know you walk beside me*
> *On the earth beneath my feet*
> *And though you're only a memory*
> *You still give to me*
> *A reason to remember*
> *And a reason to believe*
>
> *And the love that you gave me*
> *Is the reason I feel*
> *Why the heart needs affection*
> *And the soul needs the peace*

> > *RITA enters as though she is coming off stage. She is wearing a big red hat. NEIL and BETTY come to meet her.*

BETTY   That was great, Rita.

NEIL   Thought I'd feel outta place at a Women's Day thing but it wasn't half bad.

BETTY   The audience was really into it.

NEIL   I liked that song about your mother.

RITA   Thanks.

NEIL   Be nice if you'd do one in Gaelic though.

RITA   I write my own songs, Dad. I don't know Gaelic.

NEIL   Wouldn't kill you to learn one.

    RITA and BETTY laugh.

BETTY   Nice hat, by the way.

RITA   Oh, I got it for a dollar at Neighbourhood Services. With the hat I don't need a beer to help get me out there. That's what I'm working on. It's gotta be just me out there.

NEIL   You didn't look scared to me.

RITA   Once the audience starts responding I could stay all night. And those musicians. I'm so used to singing a capella it was great working with the band. It all just felt right. Something about the hometown crowd. They seem to "get me" now.

BETTY   That Judy Gould really wants to start a band with you.

RITA   She said if I moved home we could start doing the bars and stuff.

BETTY   It's awful nice having you around.

NEIL   Yuh.

RITA   I don't know.

NEIL   Yes you do, Rita.

    Lights cross to SINGER.

SINGER   *(sings "Home I'll Be")*

> *I see the mountains, feel the salt air*
> *I have reasons to behold*
> *All the wonders that never cease to be*
> *You're as timeless as the water*
> *You're as gentle as the fields*
> *I caress you oh Cape Breton in my dreams*

    Lights cross to RITA and NEIL.

NEIL   How'd your concert at the Savoy go?

RITA	Only about twenty people but it was great. I just had fun.
NEIL	Sorry I didn't make it.
RITA	'T's all right.
NEIL	Betty was saying ya got a few new songs. Even wrote one about the mines.
RITA	Since I moved home they've just been pouring out of me. I try to have some new stuff for each audience. We've almost got enough for the album.
NEIL	So that's happenin' is it?
RITA	Yeah. Funding's all in place. We start recording in November. And I met with that manager in Halifax.
NEIL	Yeah?
RITA	He's got some big plans. Thinks he might be able to get me a few weeks at Expo '86. Even wants me to shoot a pilot for a variety series.
NEIL	That's good. Real good. *(beat)* David's sure done a nice job on that house, hasn't he?
RITA	Yes, it's beautiful.
NEIL	I couldn'a done any better myself.
RITA	It's nice.
NEIL	No chance you'll be moving in with him then?
RITA	No, Dad.
NEIL	Got that big place all to himself.
RITA	He's selling it.
NEIL	Oh, I didn't know. Shame.
RITA	It just didn't work out with us, Dad. But me and the kids are doing great.
NEIL	Marriage ain't easy, Rita. You gotta work at it. Look at me and your mother. We never had it easy. We just…

sometimes life is hard and you take it out on the ones you care about the most. She's been gone ten years and there ain't a day goes by I don't feel like I lost my best friend. That's what comes from thirty-five years of marriage. That's all I want for you. A chance to have that kind of happiness. *(beat)* She'd be real proud of all your singing, you know. Me too. I mean, I am.

RITA   Thanks.

> *RITA moves in to hug him. He backs away, uncomfortably.*

NEIL   That was mostly what I wanted to say, I guess. It's nice to have you home.

RITA   It's nice to be home.

NEIL   Yeah, well, I better get back to the house. Let the dog out.

> *NEIL leaves the house and walks through the woods as lights come up on the SINGER.*

SINGER   *(cont'd "Home I'll Be")*

> *And you never let the hard times*
> *Take away your soul*
> *And you stopped the tears from falling*
> *As you watched the young ones go*
> *You're as peaceful as a clear day*
> *You're as rugged as the seas*
> *I caress you oh Cape Breton in my dreams*
>
> *And home I'll be*
> *Home I'll be*
> *Banish thoughts of leaving*
> *Home I'll be*

> *Lights cross to RITA's kitchen. She is sitting reading a newspaper. She looks at it in disbelief and throws it to the ground. She is on the verge of tears. She picks up a suitcase, opens it and starts unpacking, throwing her clothes on the floor.*

> *BETTY enters carrying a book.*

BETTY   Hey, what's going on in here?

RITA   *(pointing to the paper)* Read that.

BETTY   *(picking paper up off floor)* What?

RITA   There, in the entertainment section. "Fat Lady With Cleft Lip Not Marketable."

BETTY   Oh, Rita.

RITA   Looks like they're not picking up the series.

> *Pause.*

Nice way to find out, hunh?

BETTY   Somebody should've at least called or something.

RITA   I know it was just a pilot, there was no guarantee, but this is how I find out? I'm too fat to have a TV show. Just because you're overweight, does it mean you shouldn't be seen? Shouldn't sing, shouldn't have a dream? It's so sad that that's the way they see the world 'cause there really is a lot more to life. "Fat lady with cleft lip." *(beat)* I'm not going to Vancouver.

BETTY   You have to.

RITA   Why, so I can read, "Fat Lady Wows 'Em at Expo!"?

BETTY   Rita, you can't take it to heart. They want to sell papers. They're just looking for a catchy headline. They don't know you.

RITA   I keep thinking someday it'll all be easy. You know, it'll all come together and everything'll be smooth sailing.

BETTY   Things are going really well, Rita.

RITA   I know, I know. I'm doing my music and I'm making a living.

BETTY   If you wanted easy you wouldn't have chosen this life. You question things. That's what you do. You think about everything, then you put it down in songs for the rest of us.

RITA   Why can't they get it? Forget about the weight. Forget about the lip. I'm a singer. I sing and I write songs. I have a dream and I'm darn well living it.

BETTY   Exactly! You're living your dream. Do you know how few people can say that?

RITA   *(reluctantly agreeing)* I know.

BETTY   So get that suitcase packed and get yourself to Vancouver.

RITA   But I wanna be mad right now.

BETTY   Well go ahead and be mad. Get pissed off. But don't give up, Rita. A lot of good stuff's happening. There's bound to be some bad too. You just gotta keep on keeping on.

RITA   *(convincing herself)* Keep on keeping on.

BETTY   There you go. *(beat)* You made a hell of a mess here, though.

     BETTY starts picking up the clothes.

RITA   Leave it. I made it, I'll clean it up.

BETTY   You sure?

RITA   Yeah.

BETTY   Okay, I'll come get you in about an hour. *(She starts out, then remembers the book she brought over.)* Oh, right. *(handing it to RITA)* Look what I found when I was cleaning out some stuff.

RITA   The Stephen Foster songbook!

BETTY   I haven't seen it in years.

RITA   *(looking through the book)* This book. *(She sings.)* "Beautiful dreamer, wake unto me…" I really thought someday I'd be living in one of those pictures.

BETTY   You can keep it.

RITA   Really?

BETTY   Yeah. *(beat)* You sure you're all right?

RITA   Yeah. I am.

BETTY   Back in a bit.

RITA   Okay.

> BETTY leaves. We hear "Flying On Your Own" on guitar as RITA goes into the woods with the Stephen Foster book.

You know what, Mom? I'm gonna be okay.

> RENE appears.

RENE   You've got your music. It's part of you now. The dream is coming true. I can see it.

RITA   I wish you were really here to see it.

RENE   So many people are with you and behind you.

RITA   Sometimes it feels like I'm out there alone.

RENE   Maybe on your own, but you're never alone.

RITA   I know. In my heart, I know.

RENE   Keep dreaming, sweetie, and you'll fly. I guarantee it.

RITA   And you know what's so nice about flying?

RENE   What?

RITA   It's always sunny once you get above the clouds.

RENE   Is it ever.

> RITA sits and opens the Stephen Foster songbook. Lights up on the SINGER. RITA listens.

SINGER   *(sings "Flying On Your Own," directly to RITA)*

You were never more strong girl
You were never more alone

Once there was two, now there's just you
You're flying on your own

> RITA *closes the songbook. For the first time in the play*
> *she looks directly at the* SINGER.

RITA   (*sings*)

You were never more happy girl
You were never oh so blue
Once heartaches begin, nobody wins
You're flying on your own

> *They come together.*

RITA & SINGER

And when you know the wings you ride
Can keep you in the sky
There isn't anyone holding back you
First you stumble, then you fall
You reach out and you fly
There isn't anything you can't do

> *Full band in. Song builds to a big finish.*

You were never more wise girl
You were never more a fool
Once you break through
It's all up to you
You're flying on your own

You were never more together
You were never more apart
Once pieces of you were all that you knew
You're flying on your own

First you stumble, then you fall
You reach out and you fly
There isn't anything you can't do

> *Blackout.*

> THE END

> ENCORE – *Full cast sings "Working Man"*

Rita MacNeil (Composer/Lyricist): Born to Rene and Neil MacNeil in 1944, Rita MacNeil grew up in the tiny hamlet of Big Pond in Cape Breton, Nova Scotia. *Born A Woman*, her first album, was released with the help of friends in 1975. She gained a following on the folk-festival circuit and in the women's movement before moving home to Cape Breton in the late 1970s. Two more albums, *Part Of The Mystery* and *I'm Not What I Seem* followed. Her appearance at Expo '86 in Vancouver was a big break for her. She went on to independently record *Flying On Your Own*. When she couldn't get any recognition from major record labels, she released the album on her own. She sold so many copies that she eventually gained the interest of Virgin Records. Since then, Rita's albums have consistently hit the gold or platinum-plus sales mark in Canada. She's had top-ten hits in the UK and Australia; and her frequent concert tours, at home and abroad, are always sellouts. She has won three Juno Awards, four Canadian Country Music Awards and received five honorary doctorates. She was inducted into the Order of Canada in 1992. MacNeil is also a TV favourite. Her 1993 Christmas special, "Once Upon A Christmas," drew two million viewers and her weekly CBC-TV musical variety show, "Rita & Friends" (1994-1997), winner of a 1996 Gemini Award, drew one million viewers weekly over three seasons. Her candid autobiography *On A Personal Note* (1998, Key Porter Books) was also a national bestseller.

Photo by George Georgakakos

Charlie Rhindress is a co-founder and former artistic director of Live Bait Theatre in Sackville, New Brunswick. All eight of his full-length plays have premiered at Live Bait. *The Maritime Way of Life* has been produced in all four Atlantic Canadian provinces and was nominated for a Canadian Comedy Award as best new play in 2000. It was also published in *Marigraph: Gauging the Tides of Drama from New Brunswick/Nova Scotia/Prince Edward Island* (Playwrights Canada Press), an anthology of Maritime plays. After premiering at Live Bait, *Flying On Her Own* was produced by Neptune Theatre, and *Home and Away*, a musical about hockey co-written with Dean Burry, played at Theatre Orangeville. In addition to his full-length plays, Charlie has written over thirty dinner theatres with Karen Valanne and two plays for teens, which have been produced throughout North America. Charlie has also worked as an actor in film and at theatres across the country. He has directed for a number of East Coast theatres and served as director and dramaturge on Cathy Jones's one woman show, *Me, Dad and The Hundred Boyfriends*. Charlie is currently the interim director of the Neptune Theatre School and is working on new plays for Ship's Company Theatre, Neptune Theatre and Mulgrave Road Theatre. More importantly, he is the father of four incredible children.